1

Building Character through Picture Books

25 Family Devotions Based on Favorite Picture Books

By Terrie Hellard-Brown

Artwork by Katerina Davidenko

All scripture is taken from the ERV (Easy-to-Read Version) of the Holy Bible
Copyright © 2006 by Bible League International

This book is dedicated to
Kathi Lipp
for giving me the idea to combine my love for picture books
and my joy in writing devotionals. You're a great coach and a
wonderful friend.
And to my family who supports my picture book addiction
and enjoys them with me:
my husband Dave,
our children
Rachelle, Nate, Annalyssa, and Ryan

Thank you to artist
Katerina Davidenko
for her adorable artwork.

Table of Contents

Alexander and the Terrible, Horrible, No Good, Very Bad Day
by Judith Viorst

"At school Mrs. Dickens liked Paul's picture of the sailboat better than my picture of the invisible castle. At singing time she said I sang too loud. At counting time she said I left out sixteen. Who needs sixteen? I could tell it was going to be a terrible, horrible, no good, very bad day."

Brothers and sisters, continue to think about
what is good and worthy of praise.
Think about what is true and honorable and right and pure and
beautiful and respected. (Philippians 4:8, ERV)

The Story: Alexander is not having a good day at all. Throughout the story, he complains about all the terrible things that happen to him. He has decided that he is going to have a terrible, horrible, no good, very bad day, and he does.

We can have terrible, horrible, no good, very bad days too, especially if all we focus on is the frustrations and inconveniences of the day. God doesn't want us to live like that. The Bible tells us to focus on what is good and true.

Think About It:
1. Did Alexander have some bad things happen in his day?
2. Did he have a good reason to be upset and frustrated at times?
3. Did he cause his day to be worse by anything he did?
4. If you're having a bad day, what would happen if you focused on good things instead of the bad things?
5. What are some good things you can always think about?
6. Instead of being sad or mad about the bad things that happen in your day, what attitude could you have about the good things that happen in your day?

Do everything without complaining or arguing.
(Philippians 2:14, ERV)

For Further Thought:
1. Do you think every day has some good and some bad in it?
2. How does our attitude affect our day?
3. Can we find good things to think about while still admitting some things went wrong or that we could have done some things better? Or should we pretend everything is good? Why or why not?

Prayer for Today: Dear Jesus, sometimes I have bad days where everything seems to go wrong. You tell us in the Bible that we should think about what is true and honorable and not to complain. Help me to think about the things I should do. Help me to be thankful for all the good things in my life. You have blessed me and my family in so many ways. Thank you for caring for us and always being with us even through the bad days and the hard times. In Jesus' name, amen.

For Parents: We want to raise thankful, joyful children who can look beyond the little daily frustrations and choose to see the blessings in their lives. We need to practice this habit with them. We also need to be real. Sometimes irritations happen. We can acknowledge them without dwelling on them. We can forgive the

10

person and move on. Forgiveness sets us and the other person free from being trapped in that disagreement or hurt. Reconciliation brings relief and joy. Gratitude helps us focus on the wonderful blessings God has given us. Patience helps us wait for the good in the frustrations. However, one thing we notice throughout this story of Alexander is that many of the adults in his life ignore the truly wrong things that happen to him. Maybe the mom should have noticed the older brothers constantly picking on Alexander. Or maybe she should have helped him find some shoes he really liked. Maybe the teacher should have talked to Alexander about doing the assignment rather than pretending to do it and only turning in a blank page or discussed that participation in singing doesn't mean singing so loud one becomes obnoxious.

Several teachable moments were overlooked in Alexander's day. If we can grasp those rather than hurrying through and missing them, we can help our kids find the joy and peace of life. We can help them rest in the security of their relationship with God.

Because by Mo Willems

"In row C, seat 14—sat the girl with the uncle's ticket. She heard the beautiful music written by the man named Franz—and it changed her."

We should think about each other to see how we can encourage each other to show love and do good works. (Hebrews 10:24, ERV)

All of you together are the body of Christ. Each one of you is a part of that body. (1 Corinthians 12:27, ERV)

The Story: In this story a little girl winds up going to a symphony with her aunt because her uncle has a cold and can't use his ticket. Each person in the story has an important role to play for all the "Becauses" to happen.

What would happen if someone did not do what they were supposed to do—what would happen if the helpers did not prepare the music hall? What would happen if the ushers didn't open the doors? What would happen if the musicians didn't practice? Each person has a job and a purpose in that job.

God works life out so that each person's purpose helps to bring about His purposes. We each have a part in His plan. We each have a job to do. Someday we will see the "Because" in God's plan too.

Think About It:
1. Which person would you most like to be in this story? Why?
2. Whose job is most important in this story?
3. God gives each of us a job to do to be part of the Church. He says the church is like a body where each part has its job. What happens when each part of your body works well?
4. What happens when one part doesn't do what it's supposed to?

5. If everyone does their part, the church blesses people, and God's will is done. Do you think God is happy when everyone does their part?

6. When each person does their part in the story, what happens to others in the story?

7. We never know how God is going to use our lives. We must simply obey Him and His word. In doing that, we help people know Jesus.

Everything you say and everything you do
should be done for Jesus your Lord.
(Colossians 3:17a, ERV)

We know that in everything God works for the good of those who love
him. These are the people God chose, because that was his plan.
(Romans 8:28, ERV)

For Further Thought:

1. In this story we see some other important points: sharing can change a life. How can sharing change lives?

2. Have you ever shared something with someone? How did they react?

3. We also see that music is powerful—it speaks to our hearts in special ways.

4. Do you like music? Why or why not?

5. Do you like to use music to worship God?

Prayer for Today: Dear Jesus, show me when you want me to share something I have with someone else or do something to bless someone. I know that You have a plan. I want to be a part of what You are doing. Thank You for using people and music to bless our lives. Thank you for the people at my church and in my family who help me and bless me. In Jesus' name, amen.

13

For Parents: I love this story so much. It emphasizes the importance of being responsible in our jobs, but it also shows how each person has a purpose, and God has a plan for each person. What a great lesson for us to help our children understand. Some scriptures you may want to share with your children as you discuss this truth: Eph. 2:10, 1 Peter 4:10-11, Mark 9:41. This is also a great book to use Romans 8:28 to show that even though the uncle was sick, God still used him. And each person, no matter how small their job or how seemingly unimportant, all jobs are truly important. Every person can help make everything work together well. And when we do our part, we can change someone's life.

We can use an object lesson to help drive home the concept of each person serving a purpose by baking together. When we bake cookies, for instance, we put a little salt, a little baking powder, and a little vanilla into the mix. What if we made some cookies without one of those? What if we made cookies without sugar? How fun it is to make a few batches of cookies, one with all the ingredients, one without the baking powder, and one without the sugar. The taste test will quickly show the importance of each ingredient.

Caps for Sale by Esphyr Slobodkina

"This made the peddler angry, so he shook both hands at them and said, 'You monkeys, you! You give me back my caps.'
"But the monkeys only shook both their hands back at him and said, 'Tsz, tsz, tsz.'"

Do any of you need wisdom? Ask God for it.
He is generous and enjoys giving to everyone.
So he will give you wisdom.
(James 1:5, ERV)

The Story: In the story, the peddler ran into a problem. The monkeys took all his caps while he was sleeping. He needed to figure out how to get his caps back, but because of their copying him and not listening to him, he just kept getting angrier and angrier.

The Bible tells us if we lack wisdom, we should ask God for it. He will help us. If we find ourselves, like the peddler, in a situation where we need to solve a problem, but we are starting to get angry or frustrated instead, we should stop and pray. We should ask God to help us think clearly and ask Him for the wisdom and understanding to be able to solve the problem.

Think About It:
1. What do you do when you start to get angry?
2. How did the peddler solve his problem in the story?
3. Did he know his reaction would solve the problem?
4. If he had realized that the monkeys copied everything he did, do you think he could have solved the problem sooner instead of getting so angry?

.

Anger does not help you live the way God wants.
(James 1:20, ERV)

When you are angry, don't let that anger make you sin,"
and don't stay angry all day.
(Ephesians 4:26, ERV)

For Further Thought:
1. Have you ever noticed when you start getting angry, it is hard to think of good ideas to solve a problem?
2. We know anger is a feeling, an emotion. When does anger become a sin?
3. What would you tell someone who gets angry easily?

Prayer for Today: Dear Jesus, give me wisdom. Help me to not become angry but to find good solutions and positive answers instead. I pray that You would help me be a wise problem-solver instead of getting upset by problems I face. Thank You for helping me and giving me Your wisdom and understanding. In Jesus' name, amen.

For Parents: Anger can be a big emotion for children to process. They may not know appropriate ways to deal with their anger. They may not be able to use their words to express their anger, and, therefore, they react in ways that can hurt themselves or others. Talking about anger and feelings can help them learn the words to use. Practicing how to talk about their anger and how to find a solution without acting out will help equip them for the next time they get angry. Helping them to deal with these big emotions more calmly can also help them learn to problem-solve and think critically rather than just be blinded by their anger.

In addition, we can help them learn to problem-solve and think critically by giving them different word problems to solve. Helping them think through "what if" scenarios can help them prepare for when they find situations in real life that need them to respond calmly and with thoughtfulness.

A very hard lesson for us to learn is recognizing we cannot control others, especially if they are monkeys! Helping our children understand that they can only learn to control themselves and how they respond to situations will help them feel some power and control in what may feel is a hopeless/helpless situation. Just like in the story, when they do what they are supposed to do, things usually tend to settle down and work out.

Chicka Chicka Boom Boom
by Bill Martin Jr. and John Archambault

"A is out of bed, and this is what he said, 'Dare double dare, you can't catch me. I'll beat you to the top of the coconut tree.'"

Some friends are fun to be with,
but a true friend can be better than a brother.
(Proverbs 18:24, ERV)

The Story: *Chicka Chicka Boom Boom* is a funny story. Don't you love it? The little letters follow each other up the coconut tree and fall down hurting themselves. Even after falling down, the little letters climb the tree again. It's a silly story of choosing to follow a leader into trouble.

The letters in the story weren't afraid of climbing the coconut tree even after they fell and got a little hurt. They just climbed up again. Sometimes it's good to get up and try again when we fail or fall down. But should we keep following someone who leads us into trouble?

The Bible teaches us to follow wisely. We should choose good friends who will help us make good choices, and we are to listen to our parents and others who know what is best for us.

Think About It:

1. Maybe little letters don't get too hurt when they fall out of a coconut tree. But what would happen to you if you climbed up a coconut tree and fell out?

2. Who should we follow in life?

3. God has created us to be people who need other people. We love having friends. What does "being a good friend" mean to you?

Be friends with those who are wise, and you will become wise.
Choose fools to be your friends, and you will have trouble.
(Proverbs 13:20, ERV)

For Further Thought:

1. Who are your best friends, and why do you like them so much?
2. What can you do when friends try to get you to make bad choices?
3. What is wisdom?
4. How can we choose wisdom over bad decisions?

Prayer for Today: Dear Jesus, thank you for good friends who love you. Help me to be a good friend who chooses to be wise. Help me to follow You daily and to choose good friends I can trust. In Jesus' name, amen.

For Parents: While our children are young, we can help determine who their friends are, at least somewhat. We can talk about how to choose loyal and trustworthy friends. As they get older, keeping the conversation open with each other and talking about their friends sets the foundation for them to continue to be open with us as they become teens and grow into young adulthood. We want to create an atmosphere where our children, whatever their age, know that they can talk to us about anything and any relationship. When talking with them, we need to try to ask open-ended questions to get them talking more, and we need to affirm that we trust our kids to make good choices especially as they get older. Most of all, we need to pray for our kids and teach them what the Bible teaches about friendships and how friends influence each of us. Talking openly about how, during certain times of their lives, they will want to listen to their friends more than they do to anyone else. Encouraging them to think about what their friends are trying to get them to do and thinking for themselves are values we want to build in our children's lives.

As parents, the biggest advice we need to heed is in those times when our children are choosing to listen to their friends, we must fight the urge to criticize their friends. In fact, the more we can be kind of moms and dads to those kids, the better. Some of their friends are going to have the most irritating ideas that we want to just tell them are wrong, but we must hold on to what is most important and pick our battles wisely. Pray and pray some more especially during their teens and early twenties. We need God's wisdom and guidance. We need to keep our hearts and minds focused on keeping the conversation going and being able to introduce their friends to the Gospel. It's a challenge, but it is also a joy to see these young people begin to ask questions about our faith. It is even more wonderful when our children are the ones sharing their faith with their friends. We cannot protect them from conflicting ideas, but we can prepare our children to think critically and to know what we believe and why.

Corduroy by Don Freeman

"Recently, though, Violet found herself alone at the table. Her family had become busy. Very busy. They had found new places to be."

The Lord GOD says, "I myself will be their Shepherd.
I will search for my sheep and take care of them.
(Ezekiel 34:11, ERV)

The Story: The little girl named Lisa saw Corduroy bear in the store, and even though he had a button missing, she loved him and wanted to take him home. She saved her money so she could go back to the store and pay for him and take him home. He always wanted a home.

Jesus does the same thing for us, doesn't He? Even though we have sinned and disobeyed the Bible, Jesus loves us and paid for our sin on the cross. He wants us to be His friends.

Think About It:
1. How does it make you feel to know that Jesus wants you to be His friend?
2. How do you think Corduroy felt when Lisa chose him?
3. We talk about "being saved." What does that mean?
4. Do you have any questions about "being saved" or "becoming a Christian"?

But you are his chosen people, the King's priests.
You are a holy nation, people who belong to God.
He chose you to tell about the wonderful things he has done.
He brought you out of the darkness of sin into his wonderful light.
(1 Peter 2:9, ERV)

For Further Thought:

1. The Bible says we become God's children and friends when we believe in Jesus, when we believe He died and rose again. What does it mean to "believe" in Jesus?

2. Can we do good things to make Jesus love us more?

3. Who cannot become a Christian? Is there anyone who is "too bad" to be able to be forgiven by Jesus?

4. What does it mean to repent of our sin?

5. In the story, belonging to Violet and living in her house was all Corduroy ever wanted but didn't really know he wanted. How does becoming part of God's family give us everything we ever wanted even though we may not have realized it was all we wanted?

Prayer for Today: Dear Jesus, I believe that You are God's Son who died for my sin and rose again alive. Forgive me for my sin, and please be the Lord of my life. Please save me and help me follow You all my life. I love You so much and thank You for making me Your child and friend. In Jesus' name, amen.

-Or-

Dear Jesus, I'm learning that You want us to be your children and your friends. I pray that You will help me understand what it means to follow You and to believe in You. I still have questions, and I pray You help me understand more about You and Your plan. In Jesus' name, amen.

For Parents: Sometimes it feels like we're holding our breath as parents waiting for our children to pray that prayer and profess their faith in Christ. Then, we can breathe this sigh of relief. All will be well. They are saved.

A few things to remember:

When children start asking questions about salvation, stop and answer those questions. You may think they are too young, but I'm always surprised by how young children can be when they start their faith journey with Christ. So, answer the questions. Check for understanding. Pray with them each step of the way.

Salvation may be a "one and done" situation for some kids in that they come to a place of understanding they need a Savior, they truly open up their hearts in repentance, and from that day on, they walk with Christ. There may be some days of rebellion and repentance, but overall, their faith is solid from that day on. However, some children grow into salvation, and it is actually hard to tell where they actually "become a Christian" because they seem to understand it little by little, believing step by step. Both are valid ways of coming to Christ. Look at Paul and Peter in the Bible. Paul had an encounter that changed his life from that day on. Peter believed something from the day he left his fishing boat, but he couldn't completely profess his faith in Jesus until after the Resurrection. He confessed that Jesus was the Messiah before his death, yet he wasn't a faithful follower until after the Resurrection, and after the Holy Spirit came to them in the upper room. We watch his faith growing throughout the Gospels until we see the bold preacher in Acts. Our children, especially the ones who start believing at a very young age often grow into their faith in a similar way. They believe more as they understand more.

Discipleship begins from day one in our children's lives before they have any idea of their need for a Savior. You are building the truth into their lives each time you speak about God, show your faith, and read or pray with them.

Each child's faith journey is their faith journey. It is a living, real relationship with a living, real God. It's sometimes hard to watch all they wrestle with, but we can be there for them, pray constantly for them, and keep the doors open for conversations that can help them find their way. I firmly believe these early decisions and steps of faith are real unless we push, or people manipulate them by fear to make "a profession of faith." Let them make the baby steps and the big steps of faith in Jesus, and they will return to it even if they walk away for a time at some point in their lives.

I can't admonish you enough to keep them in church. Even if they don't want to go to church, tell them when they are adults, they can choose. But while they are young, you are responsible before God to guide them and take them to church. Make sure you are in a strong, Bible-teaching church and that their teachers are strong followers of Christ. Seeds are being planted, and their faith is being affected by these decisions we make for them.

Enemy Pie by Derek Munson

"He talked quietly, 'There is one part of Enemy Pie that I can't do. In order for it to work, you need to spend a day with your enemy. Even worse, you have to be nice to him. It's not easy. But that's the only way that Enemy Pie can work. Are you sure you want to go through with this?'"

"I'm telling you to love your enemies
and do good to them. Lend to people
without expecting to get anything back.
If you do this, you will have a great reward.
You will be children of the Most High God.
Yes, because God is good even to the
people who are full of sin and not thankful.
(Luke 6:35, ERV)

The Story: What's the best way to get rid of an enemy? That's right! Make them into a friend. The boy in the story didn't realize that was what his dad had in mind, but his dad was very smart. He knew if he spent time with Jeremy Ross and got to know him, he might get rid of an enemy.

The Bible challenges us to love our enemies, to bless them. We can pray for them as well. Many times, we just need to talk to people to understand them more and to learn that we like them or that we have common interests.

Think About It:
1. Do you think God had the idea of making friends out of our enemies in mind when He commanded us to bless our enemies?
2. Can you think of ways you could bless someone who doesn't want to be your friend? How can you love them?
3. When you're having a hard time with someone, do you find it difficult to pray for God to bless that person? If you forgave the person, would you find it easier to pray for God to bless that person?

25

Good people ask the LORD to bless others. They ask God, their
Savior, to do good things.
(Psalm 24:5, ERV)

For Further Thought:
1.   Sometimes we just cannot make an enemy into a friend. Why does God still want us to pray for them and bless them?
2.   What does that do in our hearts and minds?
3.   What should we do when we can't seem to let go of our hurt and anger?
4.   What if we can't seem to forgive someone? What can we do?

Prayer for Today: Dear Jesus, I know You say we should love our enemies, but sometimes that is really hard. Help me to be able to do it. Help me to forgive those who have been mean to me or who have hurt me. Help me to find ways to bless them. Thank you. In Jesus' name, amen.

For Parents: This is a hard lesson for all of us. Blessing someone who has hurt us or our children can be more challenging for us as parents than for our kids. We set the tone and the example for our children. They pick up on our anger and unforgiveness. They learn our prejudices and fears. We need to be careful and aware of our own feelings toward others. We need to let the Holy Spirit search our hearts and renew our minds so that we can genuinely love our enemies and bless them. In this our children can see our example, and maybe even our struggle and determination, to obey God's word and to either make friends of our enemies or to forgive them and bless them even when we cannot be friends. We can learn to live at peace with others even if they are not our friends (Romans 12:18; Matthew 22:37-39).

Because this is a difficult subject, we may need to practice some scenarios with our kids. In addition, we may want to help them learn the difference between being friends with someone we consider an enemy and forgiving someone who is not safe to try to be friends with.

Sometimes they may not like someone because that person "stole" their best friend or took their place on a team. We can talk about how to say kind things to this child and how to pray to ask God to help us forgive and be kind. However, if an adult is in their life or a truly dangerous bully, we want to help them forgive and pray for that person, but we may not want them to try to befriend this person.

As we know, kids tend to live in a black and white reality – strangers are people they don't know, so they avoid anyone they don't know, seeing them as dangerous. Or we try to teach them to be friendly and kind, so they treat everyone like a friend and trust everyone. They have a hard time discerning a stranger who is someone they can trust and one they should be wary of.

This same black and white attitude can affect how they view enemies thinking they need to try to become friends with every person they consider an enemy. Honestly, usually children can discern an adult that is untrustworthy, but we often hurt that when we force them to be kind to that person. They may think that being kind means we trust that person. So, we need to try to help them understand "Kindness to everyone. Trust and friendship for those we can trust."

Additionally, as we are teaching these lessons, I whole-heartedly believe we should never force a child to act in a certain way when they do not feel it. Again, we can teach them to be kind. They do not need to be disrespectful to the weird uncle they don't trust. But we do not need to force them to kiss him goodbye or sit on his lap. If they are getting a creepy feeling, let them act in a cautious way toward that person. Let them keep their distance.

Flashlight by Lizi Boyd

Later, Jesus talked to the people again. He said, "I am the light of the world. Whoever follows me will never live in darkness. They will have the light that gives life." (John 8:12, ERV)

The Story: This is a wordless book, but the pictures tell such a fun story of a little boy who shines his flashlight into the darkness. In the light, the boy can see clearly the animals around him, and any fear disappears.

The Bible talks about light and darkness. It says that Jesus is the Light of the world--. It says that we should share His light with others. Just like light showed the boy in the story what was really around him, Jesus, as the Light of the World, shines Truth in our hearts and lives. He helps us to know we need a Savior, and that He is our only Hope.

Think About It:
1.   What did the little boy see when he shined his flashlight into the dark?
2.   Was he afraid?
3.   What happened when he didn't shine the light where he was walking?
4.   When a light shines, what happens to the darkness?
5.   What does it mean for Jesus to say He is the Light of the world?

In the same way, you should be a light for other people. Live so that they will see the good things you do and praise your Father in heaven. (Matthew 5:16, ERV)

For Further Thought:
1.   How can we share Jesus' light with the world?
2.   When people look at your life, do they see Jesus' light?
3.   What are ways you could share His light more?
4.   How does Jesus' light help you walk through life?

Prayer for Today: Jesus, I'm so glad You are the Light of the world. Thank You for shining Your light and helping me see how You need to forgive me. Your light gives me peace, joy, and, most of all, Your love. Please help me shine Your light to my friends and others around me. In Jesus' name, amen.

For Parents: We don't often think of light as a character trait we want our kids to have, but being light means reflecting God's character, living out the fruit of the Spirit in our lives, and doing good deeds. Helping our children strive to do good to others and to let God's Spirit work through them is something we can help our children understand.

I like to use an object lesson with this idea. We talk about what God is like, and then we talk about how we reflect God's love and light to the world. Using a candle or flashlight and a mirror, children can move the mirror around the room reflecting the light source.

Then we can discuss what we can do to reflect God's light.

Fly! By Mark Teague

Children, obey your parents in everything. This pleases the Lord.
(Colossians 3:20, ERV)

The Story: In the story *Fly!* The mom tells the baby bird what he needs to do and why. He argues and makes jokes. Mama bird gets more serious and warns the baby bird of the dangers of disobeying her.

The baby bird is obviously able to fly. Notice he flew down when he fell out of the tree. He is old enough to find his own worms. He is old enough to fly south for the winter. But he doesn't want to obey his mom. He wants his mom to do everything for him.

God tells us in the Bible that if we love Him, we will obey Him. He also tells us to obey our parents.

Think About It:
1. What did the mama bird want the baby bird to do? Why?
2. What did the baby bird want to do? Was it wise?
3. Why did he finally decide to obey?
4. When we obey our parents, who is happy?
5. When was a time you were glad you obeyed your parents? Why were you glad?
6. When was a time you wish you had obeyed your parents but didn't? Why do you wish you had obeyed?

"If you love me, you will do what I command. (John 14:15, ERV)

For Further Thought:
1. Why do you think God commands us to obey our parents and Him?
2. How does obedience show we love our parents and God?
3. Have you ever wanted your mom or dad to do things for you that you know you could do for yourself? Do you think that is a good choice?
4. Is it better to obey out of love or fear? Why?

Prayer for Today: Dear Jesus, Thank You for the Bible to teach me the right way to live. I know You care for me, and You've given me my parents to help me learn the right ways. I pray You help me obey. Help me want to obey and to see the wisdom in obedience. In Jesus' name, amen.

For Parents: Notice that the mama bird tries to encourage the child to obey by telling him the benefits and why it's important, but she doesn't use the most dangerous reason until necessary. It is important to note, we don't want to scare our children or shock them. We want them to obey out of love and trust for us. We want them to obey because we told them to. But sometimes they need to know what happens when they disobey and why obedience is important.

We should be careful not to fall into the tactics of threat, guilt-trip, danger of actions because of frustration or anger. Sometimes our children need to know the full picture, but they don't always need to know all the consequences of what could happen. If we can teach our children true discipline, most of the time they will obey because it is the right thing to do and not because we've frightened them into obedience. True discipline comes from within our own hearts and minds. That is our goal as parents—to help our children find this type of self-discipline.

One of the statements we taught our children is "Obeying is acting without arguments, excuses, or hesitation." We also told them they could question or discuss the directive once they are in the process of obeying. They were always allowed, when responding with respect, to ask if they could postpone the chore, for instance. But first, they needed to start obeying and show respect.

If you would like to read more about teaching discipline, one of the best books we've found is *Setting Limits* by Robert J. Mackenzie.

The Girl Who Never Made Mistakes
by Mark Pett and Gary Rubenstein

"Beatrice went to the refrigerator and carefully chose the biggest, eggiest eggs she could find. But on the way back, her legs slipped out from under her. The eggs went flying. Beatrice was about to make her first mistake. But she didn't!"

"'That was close!' thought Beatrice…For the rest of the school day, Beatrice couldn't stop thinking about her Almost Mistake."

We all make many mistakes. A person who never said anything wrong would be perfect. Someone like that would be able to control their whole body too.
(James 3:2, ERV)

The Story: Beatrice didn't usually make mistakes. She did what she was supposed to do all the time, but mistakes happen, and nobody is perfect. When she made an "Almost Mistake," she became worried about making other mistakes.

In life, we all make mistakes. We can try not to make mistakes, but we just can't be perfect on our own. Plus, we choose to sin and do things God says not to do. We can try not to sin, but the Bible tells us that we all sin. We all need Jesus to help us, forgive us, and to make us right with Him.

Think About It:
1. What is a mistake, and what is sin? What's the difference?
2. How do you feel when you make a mistake?
3. How do you feel when you sin?
4. What should you do when you make a mistake? What did Batrice do?
5. What should you do when you sin?

If we say that we have no sin, we are fooling ourselves,
and the truth is not in us.
(1 John 1:8, ERV)

For Further Thought:
1. Do you ever feel guilty when you make a mistake?
2. Have you ever made someone else feel bad for making a mistake?
3. What is a better reaction to mistakes rather than guilt or shame?
4. What should our response be when we sin?
5. What is God's promise to us when we confess our sin?
6. What is the difference between perfection and perfectionism?

Prayer for Today: Dear Jesus, I really don't like it when I mess up. I try so hard to do things right, and I still fail. I know that mistakes are just part of life. Help me to have a better attitude so that I can laugh at myself and learn from my mistakes. And, Jesus, I'm so sorry when I choose to sin against what You want me to do. Please forgive me. I want to follow You and obey. In Jesus' name, amen.

For Parents: We sometimes have a hard time accepting mistakes we make. Fear of failure can cripple us from trying new things or doing our best. Fear of looking foolish can stop us from having a great time. Helping our children learn to laugh at their mistakes and to have an attitude of learning from them is definitely a parenting challenge. Our culture loves to shame people for things that are not moral or spiritual, and we need to help our kids distinguish the difference between mistakes and sin. We also can try to equip them with the ability to measure whether they should "own" the shame or guilt being thrust upon them by others or their own consciences.

We also need to be aware of our own perfectionistic tendencies. We can burden our children with those expectations if we are not careful. In reality, perfectionism is idolatry. Only God is perfect, and only God can make us perfect through salvation. Perfectionism tells us we can make ourselves perfect, or we can become like God (I've heard that temptation somewhere before—like in the Garden of Eden).

In addition, helping children understand sin and the need for repentance and forgiveness is vital to helping them grow as disciples. Helping them understand the difference between honest mistakes and willful sin can be fairly easy if we don't shame them for mistakes.

Sometimes we need to examine our own feelings. We may be frustrated, angry, or disappointed because our children haven't been careful, and they've made some serious mistakes that broke something valuable or hurt someone we love. However, we need to keep those feelings clearly delineated from moral/spiritual failures, and, with love and kindness, help them come to a place of asking for (and accepting) forgiveness.

Grumpy Monkey by Suzanne Lang

"Are you okay?" asked Jim.

"It hurts, but I'll probably feel better soon enough," said Norman. "Are you still grumpy?"

"Yes," said Jim, "but *I'll* probably feel better soon enough too..."

When others are happy, you should be happy with them.
And when others are sad,
you should be sad too. (Romans 12:15, ERV)

The Story: In this story Norman is such a good friend to Jim, but all the animals want to help Jim feel better. When Jim was grumpy, the animals said he was all bunched up, so he tried to fake smile and un-bunch himself to look happy, but he wasn't happy. He was probably even more miserable.

God wants us to be encouragers and helpers to our friends too. We learn from Norman and from the Bible how to do that well.

Think About It:
1. How did the animals try to make Jim less grumpy?
2. What does Norman do that makes Jim feel better?
3. How would you feel if your friends tried to make you feel something different than you feel? Would it frustrate you? Hurt your feelings? Make you angry? Make you sad?
4. What if you were happy, and a friend said you were silly for being happy? Would that make you mad? Sad? Embarrassed?
5. How would you feel if a friend came and put his arm around you, hugged you, and said, "I'm sorry you are sad. Are you okay?"
6. Which kind of friend do you want to be?

Singing happy songs to a sad person is as foolish as taking a coat off
on a cold day or mixing soda and vinegar.
(Proverbs 25:20, ERV)

For Further Thought:

1.   What do you do if friends don't understand your feelings or don't let you feel what you feel?

2.   Can you be patient with them and love them?

3.   Can you acknowledge their feelings and help them even if they aren't doing a good job of helping you?

4.   Would Jesus want you to forgive them or be angry with them?

5.   What should you say to them if they've hurt your feelings?

Prayer for Today: Dear Jesus, help me to be the kind of friend who can be patient with my friends and let them feel sad, happy, or grumpy when they need to. Help me think more about their feelings instead of just thinking about how I feel, so I can be a good friend to them. In Jesus' name, amen.

For Parents: Listening. Being heard. These are tremendous gifts we give to people who are grieving or who are simply having a bad day. Helping our children practice listening is a great skill for them to learn. Helping our children feel heard is essential to their emotional health. We can help our children learn how to sit quietly and let someone talk about how they feel without adding advice or giving an opinion. This isn't always easy, but it is often very helpful to the person who is hurting.

We can teach our kids that sometimes, when a friend is sad, it is best just to sit with them and let them be sad and let them tell you how they are feeling. You can be sad with them instead of trying to make them happy. When we try to make someone feel happy, sometimes we are not really doing it for them but so that we will feel better because we are uncomfortable with our friends being sad or grumpy. But a good friend will let their friends feel what they do, and friends often feel what their friends feel too which is empathy. In fact, the Bible tells us that trying to force a person to feel happy is just silly. But it calls us to weep with those who weep and rejoice with those who rejoice as the verses above teach us.

If your child has trouble understanding how others are feeling, many books and resources exist to help us teach emotional understanding. Part of it involved learning to "read" the expressions, voice tones, and body language of others. Helping our children notice these can help them become great empathizers and comforters.

I'm Not Scared, YOU'RE Scared!
by Seth Meyers

"One day, Rabbit made an announcement. 'Bear, we are going on an adventure!'

Bear suggested that, instead of going on an adventure, they could read a book *about* adventures...Rabbit looked at her friend and asked, 'Bear, are you scared?'

And Bear replied, 'I'm not scared, *you're* scared!'"

Where God's love is, there is no fear, because
God's perfect love takes away fear.
(1 John 4:18a, ERV)

The Story: In the story, Bear is afraid of everything, and Rabbit isn't afraid of anything. But every time Bear is confronted about being afraid, he says he's not scared. And he goes and does something to get where he needs to be. At the end, however, something changes.

Jesus tells us not to be afraid. We are to be strong and courageous. We are to overcome fear and recognize is it not from God.

Think About It:
1. Are you ever scared? What do you do to get rid of your fear?
2. Why does God tell us not to be afraid?
3. What is the opposite of fear?
4. What scares you the most? Can we pray together about it?

The Spirit God gave us does not make us afraid. His Spirit
is a source of power and love and self-control.
(2 Timothy 1:7, ERV)

For Further Thought:
1. Do you ever feel so scared you panic? What do you do?
2. In the story, when Bear wasn't afraid, what could he do?
3. Rabbit wasn't scared of anything, but do you think he acted wisely?
4. How can we make wise choices but not fearful choices?
5. What does it mean that God gives us power, love, and self-control?

Prayer for Today: Dear Jesus, Sometimes I am afraid. I am so glad You do not give us a spirit of fear, but with Your help, I can be strong and courageous. When I am afraid, help me remember to trust in You. Help me to have a clear mind, and please fill me with Your Spirit of peace. In Jesus' name, amen.

For Parents: Fear is one of those struggles most of us face. As parents, it often shows up as worry and concern for our children. But whatever form it wears, fear can cripple us and hinder us from the faith we are called to. Thankfully, our faith comes from God. We can ask Him for more faith and wisdom in the circumstances we face.

One of the characteristics of fear is being contagious. Our children will learn to fear what we fear. According to what psychology says, the only fears we have innately are the fear of falling and of loud noises. I don't know if that is true or not, but I know that it doesn't take long for all kinds of fears to plague our children. And today it seems that anxiety has found a stronghold in our culture. We can help our children and ourselves find victory with the help of the Holy Spirit and God's word.

Memorize scripture or at least know scripture well allows the Spirit to bring verses back to our minds when facing difficult situations.

Pray - prayer strengthens us and reminds us that God is with us always and in all situations.

Recognize where fear is being propagated in your life – is it the news, social media, a friend who constantly shares negative ideas, or your own thought-life?

Embrace what God has given us:

Love – love guides our choices and relationships. It helps us when we are fearful to overcome assumptions and what-ifs about people around us. When love governs our expectations and reactions, we can take risks and be transparent and vulnerable.

Power – we have the power to overcome. We are meant to be more than conquerors in the struggles of life. That includes our doubts and fears that threaten to keep us from walking in peace and love. We have the power to stand in faith rather than fear, but we must choose it.

Self-control or self-discipline – we do not have to give in to the fear and anxiety of life. We can stop it at the first temptation for fear, taking every thought captive. We can choose to obey God and follow His ways regardless of what's happening in our world or in our lives. Giving up these and losing our joy makes us weak, victimized, and vulnerable to fear.

Talk to a friend, but don't just talk about your fear; talk about your faith, talk about God's word and His promises. Share together and pray together. You will both be strengthened in your faith.

Believe God. He says in our weakness He is strong. Trust Him to surprise you as you trust Him and believe His word.

Help our children with these tools as well. May God bring peace to our homes and to our children's hearts as we do.

The Invisible Boy by Trudy Ludwig

"In the cafeteria, Madison and her friends talk about her birthday party.

'The rope swing over the pool was awesome!' says J.T.

'Yeah, so was the waterslide,' adds Fiona.

'That was the best pool party ever!'

'I'm so glad you guys had fun!' says Madison. Everybody did except Brian.

He wasn't invited."

But the fruit that the Spirit produces in a person's life is love, joy, peace, patience, kindness, goodness, faithfulness, gentleness, and self-control. There is no law against these kinds of things. (Galatians 5:22-23, ERV)

The Story: In the story we see Brian being ignored or excluded many times. But he is kind anyway, and when someone is kind back to him, everything changes.

The Bible teaches us to be kind to each other and to love others.

Think About It:
1. Why do you think the book is called *The Invisible Boy?*
2. How does Brian feel each time he was ignored and excluded?
3. How would that make you feel?
4. Brian wrote a note to Justin. Why?
5. How do you think that note made Justin feel?

We show that we are God's servants by our pure lives, by our understanding, by our patience, and by our kindness. We show it by the Holy Spirit, by genuine love. (2 Corinthians 6:6, ERV)

For Further Thought:

1.   When we feel ignored and excluded, what can we do? Can we learn something from Brian?

2.   How do you choose who is on your team or in your group? Do you need to make changes in how you do those things?

3.   What is more important to you: having a winning team, working in a group with my best friends, or meeting new friends and helping others?

4.   Is it hard to try to be friends with someone everyone else is excluding? Why or why not? What could you do to make a difference in someone's life?

Prayer for Today: Dear Jesus, thank You for Your kindness to us. You did not choose favorites, and no one is ever invisible to You. That is so wonderful to realize. I know You have told us to be kind and love others. Sometimes that is hard, and sometimes it means I have to feel awkward and uncomfortable as I get to know someone new, but I pray You will help me be kinder and aware of those who are being ignored, excluded, or bullied. Help me to be kind and loving so others can see how kind and loving You are too. In Jesus' name, amen.

For Parents: One of the risks of helping our children befriend the outcast student is realizing those who reject that student may reject our children as well. They must be strong enough to handle possible teasing or even bullying. Helping our children count the cost is important but helping them see the importance of being kind is even more important. They can make such a difference in another child's life. If they start when they are young, showing kindness will just become part of who they are. As they reach the teen years when peer pressure can be brutal, they may very well find an inner strength built on the playgrounds of elementary school when they befriended the outcast.

Another aspect of this story is helping our children notice those around them. We all need to learn to be less self-absorbed in our worlds. You may want to share the scripture from Matthew 25:31-40. How can we help the "least of these" if we don't even notice they have a need? We can teach our children that a kind word, a smile, or sharing our snack with someone who forgot theirs are all little actions that can help others.

What if our child is the one who is left out or unseen? How can we help them? This is heartbreaking as a parent. We grieve for our child and the pain he or she is bearing. But we can be their safe place. We can keep the conversation open if we will let them share without trying to fix the situation or them. However, we can help them through praying with them, listening to them, and very gently challenging them to step out of their comfort zones. In the story Brian encourages others and is happy about his artistic abilities. Encouraging our children to be proactive in the same way and to find encouragement in their talents and abilities will help them find inner strength even when feeling invisible.

The Little House by Virginia Lee Burton

"The Little House was very happy as she sat on the hill and watched the countryside around her. She watched the sun rise in the morning and she watched the sun set in the evening. Day followed day, each one a little different from the one before…but the Little House stayed just the same."

I know how to live when I am poor and when I have plenty. I have learned
the secret of how to live through any kind of situation—when I have enough to
eat or when I am hungry, when I have everything I need or when I have nothing.
Christ is the one who gives me the strength I need to do whatever I must do.
(Philippians 4:12-13, ERV)

The Story: The Little House saw many changes all around her. She went from living in the beautiful countryside to being in the middle of a crowded city. But she never complained. She watched everything with curiosity. Then, in the end she had another big change when she was moved back to the countryside.

Change is hard, even when it is good change. God tells us to not complain, but to be content. He is with us, and He has a plan.

Think About It:
1. How would you describe the Little House?
2. Was she happy about all the changed happening around her?
3. Do you like when things change?
4. Are you excited for any changes coming up in your life? What changes? Why are you excited? Or why not?
5. What are some changes that you are afraid of or think you would not like?

Don't worry about anything, but pray and ask God
for everything you need, always giving thanks for what you have.
And because you belong to Christ Jesus, God's peace
will stand guard over all your thoughts and feelings.
His peace can do this far better than our human minds.
(Philippians 4:6-7, ERV)

For Further Thought:

1. What do you think it means to be content in your circumstances?

2. Does being content mean we are happy about everything happening?

3. How can we be content when we're not happy?

4. Do you think God wants us to learn something when we go through changes? What could some of those lessons be?

5. What can you do to help other family members have an easier time going through change?

6. How can you best prepare for changes?

7. Do you think it is okay to pray for something to change when you are unhappy? Why or why not?

Prayer for Today: Dear Jesus, sometimes I don't like when things change. Change can be scary and difficult. I am so thankful that You promise to always be with me, and I want to trust you and not worry about everything. Help me to be strong and peaceful whatever circumstances I'm in. In Jesus' name, amen.

For Parents: Peace and contentment are so tough for many of us. As children, we always seem to be wanting to be older or unhappy about waiting for something. As adults, we may find it difficult to walk with a peaceful, content heart when we are always busy, striving, worrying, and working to stay on top of all our responsibilities. We can work to help ourselves find contentment and share it with our children. Even in difficult times, we can find peace and stillness as we focus on God and work to understand our circumstances from His perspective rather than our limited view.

Keys to contentment:
- Praying
- Trusting God's plan
- Knowing God is with us
- Realizing "this too shall pass" in all situations
- Resting in God's presence
- Accepting my current reality

As you pray today's prayer with your children, consider having them pray specifically about any upcoming changes or challenges or any changes that they are still trying to accept.

Llama Llama Red Pajama by Anna Dewdney

"Llama llama
red pajama
in the dark
without his mama.
Eyes wide open,
covers drawn...
What if Mama Llama's GONE?"

> *God has said, "I will never leave you;*
> *I will never run away from you."*
> *(Hebrews 13:5b, ERV)*

The Story: Baby Llama thought Mama was gone. He panicked. Mama was coming, but she had things to do first. Baby Llama was impatient and worried. He wanted his mama to come to him immediately when he called.

Sometimes we can be like that when we pray to God. We ask Him to answer our prayers, and we want Him to answer them NOW! And when He waits for the right timing, we get impatient or sometimes doubt that He's still there.

Think About It:
1. Do you pray?
2. Is God ever gone?
3. When we're afraid, what should we do?
4. Do you believe God will give you everything you need?
5. Do you believe He hears all your prayers?

> *But the Lord said, "My grace is all you need. Only when you*
> *are weak can everything be done completely by my power."*
> *So I will gladly boast about my weaknesses.*
> *Then Christ's power can stay in me.*
> *(2 Corinthians 12:9, ERV)*

For Further Thought:

1.   Have you ever felt alone and afraid? What happened?

2.   Do you truly believe God is always with you? Why or why not? How does that make you feel?

3.   What questions do you have about God's grace and help?

4.   Why do you think God sometimes waits to answer our prayers?

Prayer for Today: Dear Jesus, I want to trust You. I know You say that You are always with us, but it is hard to believe when I feel alone. My feelings are so big sometimes that I believe them more than I believe what the Bible says. Help me to know and trust Your Word, and help me to stand firm in faith. I know You love me. I know You never leave me and are there even when I don't feel like You are. I know You are a good and loving Heavenly Father who meets all my needs. In Jesus' name, amen.

For Parents: Sometimes we pray and feel our prayers are simply hitting the ceiling. Nothing changes. We feel distant from God and wonder if He's even heard us. We need to help our children (and ourselves) remember that God always hears us. He is always with us. But He doesn't always answer us when we want Him to. He is wiser than we are and knows more than we do. His purposes are not our purposes. So, we trust Him. Helping our kids understand this is important. It helps them recognize that God is not some Santa figure in the sky who will give us whatever we ask for when we ask for it. He is not mean and doesn't withhold important things from us either. He knows what is best, and He wants what will help us become more like Him.

We can tell our children the truth: It's normal for us to feel like God isn't hearing us sometimes, but what we need to realize is that those feelings are telling us a lie. We are not alone. God is always with us. And He hears every single prayer we ever pray. He will answer us with the right answer because He is wise and wonderful.

We can ask questions and find out what they are afraid of or what is bothering them: Why do you think God isn't listening to your prayers? When we're afraid, what should we do? We are usually thinking about untrue things or "what if" things, like what if this happens or what if that happens. But what ifs are not real. They are our imagination. God gives us a wonderful promise. He promises that whatever happens, not only is He with us, but His grace is abundant and will help us in difficult situations. We just need to trust Him and ask for His help. He is happy to help us with whatever we are facing. Ask. Trust. Rest in Jesus.

Waiting on answers is also a time for humility before God and submission to His will. It is an opportunity to grow in our faith as we trust Him in all our circumstances. When we help our children see us walking through waiting times with patience and grace, and even allow them to see us struggle with our faith sometimes, it helps them grow and mature in their faith as well.

50

One of the things I often reiterate when teaching parents how to disciple their children is transparency. Painting an unrealistic, and untrue, picture of Christianity is not helpful to us or them. Christianity is hard. Life is hard. Waiting is really hard. We need to be honest and real with our children. Their future faith may depend on it. Many of those who are re-examining their faith are doing it because of the kind of false faith they've grown up under. Some, of course, are simply rebelling against the word of God and not wanting to submit to God, but many have been disillusioned by the reality of a hard faith that goes against the "pie in the sky" type of Christianity they were taught when they were young. Reality set in, and they didn't like it. We must not do that to our children. We must be transparent and true to the truth of God's word and the reality of following Him. We can help our children count the cost of discipleship and decide to truly follow God with their whole hearts and lives even at a young age when we are honest and genuine with them.

Miss Rumphius by Barbara Cooney

"Alice told him she would travel there and then come home to live by the sea That's all very well, he said, but there's a third thing you must do You must do something to make the world more beautiful 'All right,' said Alice, but she didn't know what that could be."

We must not get tired of doing good. We will receive our harvest of eternal life at the right time. We must not give up.
(Galatians 6:9, ERV)

The Story: Miss Rumphius is a true story of a lady who grew up, traveled the world, and made friends in many places. Her uncle told her when she was a little girl to make the world more beautiful in some way. She returned home as an older lady and had to decide how she could make the world more beautiful.

We can also make the world more beautiful. God gives us some ideas of what we can do to make a difference in the world. When we do these things, it is like planting seeds of kindness in people's lives just like Miss Rumphius planted lupine seeds wherever she went.

Think About It:

1. Do you think Miss Rumphius made the world more beautiful in others ways besides planting flowers? How?

2. What are some of the ways God tells us to make the world a better place?

3. Can you think of ways you'd like to make the world more beautiful?

Human, the LORD has told you what goodness is.
This is what he wants from you: Be fair to other people.
Love kindness and loyalty, and humbly obey your God.
(Micah 6:8, ERV)

For Further Thought:

1. From the time she was very young, Miss Rumphius had plans to see the world and then return to her hometown. Do you have plans for your future? What are they?

2. Do you think it would be fun to visit many other countries like Miss Rumphius did?

3. What would be special about making friends wherever you go?

4. What can you do today to make a positive difference in the world or to make someone's world a little more beautiful?

Prayer for Today: Dear Jesus, I think it would be wonderful to make the world a better, more beautiful place. Help me know how to do that. I want to help others and do good for others. I want to share kindness and love, and I want to obey You. I also hope you will make something beautiful out of me. In Jesus' name, amen.

For Parents: Miss Rumphius had a plan even as a little child, and she did it. She traveled the world making friends and making a difference everywhere she went. She made the world more beautiful just by loving people and experiencing their cultures with appreciation. When we do good to others, become good friends, show kindness and love, or humbly obey God, we are making the world a better, more beautiful place. We can help our children realize that doing small acts of kindness and showing love to others is powerful and can be life-changing for the other person and for the one doing the kindness. And we also are becoming more beautiful as we share God's love with the world.

And how will anyone go and tell them without being sent?
That is why the Scriptures say, "How beautiful are
the feet of messengers who bring good news!"
(Romans 10:15, NLT)

Additionally, this book and lesson opens up another opportunity for us as parents to talk about how truly beautiful God's world already is. We can take our children out into nature and see the beauty of a flower and talk about our Creator. Many books lend themselves to a nature walk and discussion, but when we talk about making the world a more beautiful place, we should start by thanking God for the beauty He's already added to this world. We are such a small part of all He's created. And yet, He cares for each of us individually. He knew us by name even before we were born. Understanding how small we are allows us to humble ourselves before the great Creator of all things, and understanding how He knows each of us personally allows us to humbly rejoice before His throne with gratitude and awe.

Olivia by Ian Falconer

"When they've finished reading, Olivia's mother gives her a kiss and says, 'You know you really wear me out. But I love you anyway.'"

Always be humble and gentle.
Be patient and accept each other with love.
(Ephesians 4:2, ERV)

The Story: Olivia is a very talented and busy pig. The book tells us that she wears out her mother because she is so busy all the time. Are you like that too? But her mother loves her and accepts her even when she makes a mess or wears out her mom.

The Bible teaches us that we are supposed to love others and accept them the way they are. We do not require people to change before we love them and care about them.

Think About It:
1. Do you find it hard to love some people sometimes? Why?
2. Have you ever asked God to help you love others.
3. When you remember that God has loved and accepted you, does that help you love others more easily?
4. When you remember God has blessed and forgiven you so much, can you learn to also love and forgive others?

Christ accepted you, so you should accept each other.
This will bring honor to God.
(Romans 15:7, ERV)

For Further Thought:

1. Is there something that came to your mind that you may be doing that irritates or wears out other people?

2. Do you think God wants you to work on choosing to behave differently in that area?

Prayer for Today: Jesus, I want to love people. Help me to love others and accept them. Help me to be creative, imaginative, and fun like Olivia in the story, but help me also to be aware if I am wearing others out. Thank you for loving me even when I am messy or make wrong choices. Forgive me when I have a bad attitude or disobey. In Jesus' name, amen.

For Parents: We can find it very challenging to help our children have empathy or to understand how they are making others feel. We talked about how to help our children "read" a person's expression or body language. However, we also need to help them take in the situation they've walked into. Kids can be so focused on their mission to get Mom's help, tattle on a sibling, or find a snack, that they don't even realize they are interrupting and disrupting situations. Sometimes role playing can help. In addition, breaking down a situation into small parts (we call that task analysis) can help children, especially young children or those on the autism spectrum. For instance, a child can pretend to be talking on the phone while you interrupt constantly. They can see how frustrating that can be. Then, we can help our children practice waiting to talk to us when we're on the phone. Breaking that down can be: 1. When you need something, you first **look** – is Mom or Dad on the phone or talking to someone else? Then, we **stop** and **wait**. 2. Is what I need to say important? Then, **tap** Mom or Dad on the arm or leg to let them know you are there. Do not say anything yet. 3. When Mom or Dad asks what you need, then you can **calmly and clearly ask or tell** them what you need to say. Practice the scenario. These activities can help children understand how their actions affect others and how to be more kind and less bothersome to adults if they tend to be a little like Olivia at times.

Our Table by Peter H. Reynolds

"Recently, though, Violet found herself alone at the table. Her family had become busy. Very busy. They had found new places to be."

The believers spent their time listening
to the teaching of the apostles.
They shared everything with each other.
They ate together and prayed together.
(Acts 2:42, ERV)

The Story: Violet remembers all the good times her family used to have around their dining room table. Now, everyone is doing other things, and she misses those times. She does what she can to help her family find each other again by making a new table and spending time together.

In the Bible God tells us to fellowship together with our Christian friends. We are busy, but it's important to spend time together. It helps us grow closer and helps us stay closer to God as well.

Think About It:

1. What do you enjoy doing together around the table with your family?

2. What are some other things besides eating that your family does around the table?

3. Do you spend time with friends from your church? What do you do together?

4. What is your favorite activity to do with your family? With your church friends?

We must not quit meeting together, as some are doing.
No, we need to keep on encouraging each other.
This becomes more and more important
as you see the Day getting closer.
(Hebrews 10:25, ERV)

For Further Thought:
1. Why does God want us to fellowship with our church friends?
2. Why is it important to spend time with our family?
3. Which is more important: your games/phone or people? Why?

Prayer for Today: Dear Jesus, I know Your plan is for us to spend time with people, with our families and with our church friends. I admit that I would sometimes rather play with my toys or games instead of spending time with people. But I am so thankful for my family and friends. Help me remember what a blessing they are and to spend more time with them. In Jesus' name, amen.

For Parents: We hear it all the time—how today's children don't even know how to interact with people because they've become addicted or enamored with electronic devices. We too can get so busy we find it hard to spend real, quality time with anyone. Cherishing the family table is so important; making it a priority in our homes and inviting church friends to join us around the table helps us find the joy of fellowship and community. We can read the Bible together at the table, and talk, talk, talk. The table is a blessing, and God's command for us to fellowship with each other is a blessing. We will find our lives enriched and our faith strengthened as we fellowship together.
1. We should make clear rules for the table and stick to them letting our children know why it is a priority.
2. We can make table time meaningful and special.
3. We should include fun times around the table – playing games, sharing jokes and riddles, or creating a family dream plan for the future or for the next vacation.

4. We can consider making a Shabbat/Sabbath time around the table each week, especially if we can include friends from church or the community as well.

5. We can include prayer, worship, and devotional time around the table. It only takes a few minutes to make it meaningful without losing the attention of our youngest ones.

God bless you as you choose to preserve this important part of building families and discipling children.

Ruby's Wish by Shirin Yim Bridges

"But most importantly," said Ruby, staring hard at her red shoes, "the boys will get to go to university, but the girls will be married."

"Don't you want to be married?" asked her grandfather. "You know, you are very lucky. A daughter of this house can marry any man."

"I know, Grandfather," said Ruby, "but I'd much rather go to university."

> *You don't get what you want because you don't ask God.*
> *Or when you ask, you don't receive anything*
> *because the reason you ask is wrong.*
> *You only want to use it for your own pleasure.*
> *(James 4:2b-3, ERV)*

The Story: This book is based on a true story of the author's grandmother Ruby. She wanted to go to university. She loved learning. But back then, girls did not go to school. Ruby could have just stayed silent. She could have kept her wish to go to college a secret. Instead, she told her grandfather her wish. And he made her wish come true.

God tells us to ask Him for what we want or need. When we learn God's word, we will ask with hearts that are right with God, and He will give us what we ask for. He will not give us answers that will hurt us or be bad for us. That's why first having our hearts right with God is so important. Then we will ask with the right attitude and mind.

Think About It:
1. What is the difference between a wish and a prayer?
2. Why does God want us to pray?
3. Why does He want us to ask for what we need and want?
4. When you pray, do you pray for others as well as yourself?
5. What does it mean to ask for the wrong reason?
6. What else do we do in prayer besides ask God for things?

Stay joined together with me and follow my teachings.
If you do this, you can ask for anything you want,
and it will be given to you.
(John 15:7, ERV)

For Further Thought:

1. Has God answered one of your prayers? Can you share about it?
2. Is any prayer too small or too big?
3. How do we know if we are praying for what we should pray for?
4. What happens if we don't pray?
5. Have you ever complained about not having something you wanted or needed only to realize you never asked God about it in prayer?
6. The Bible commands us to pray. It actually says to pray without stopping. (1 Thessalonians 5:17). Why do you think God wants us to pray about everything all the time?

Prayer for Today: Dear Jesus, thank You for telling us to pray. I am so happy that I can talk to You about everything, big or small. You promise to always hear my prayers. I can tell you I'm sorry when I do something wrong, and You forgive me. I praise You for being such a loving and amazing God, and I thank You for all You have done. Thank you for answering my prayers. I love You so much. I want to be a good pray-er. In Jesus' name, amen.

For Parents: Don't we love to hear our children pray? I know God loves hearing their prayers and ours. So often we've taught our kids to only pray for what they want. If we read the Psalms to them and help them learn to praise and honor God's name as well, how much sweeter their prayers will become. And we are building a great habit into their lives as well as planting the Word of God in their hearts. As you go through the psalms, consider sharing the psalms of lament and other emotions that we all have. During those times when our children need those words, they will be in their minds and hearts.

We start when our children are their youngest using prayer as a focus on gratitude, thanking God for our food, our family, and all His blessings. At some point, we shift to asking and interceding. After that, we add praise and worship. During the asking phase, we can teach so many important qualities to our children: continuing with a heart of gratitude, humility, respect, and patience. I think it is important to help our children think about what they are asking for. Would God want them to have what they are asking for? Also, teaching them that nothing is too big or too small for God. They never need to be afraid to ask for anything, but they need to understand that God knows best when to say yes, no, or wait.

The Runaway Bunny by Margaret Wise Brown

"Once there was a little bunny who wanted to run away.
So he said to his mother, 'I am running away.'
'If you run away,' said his mother, 'I will run after you.
For you are my little bunny.'"

"Suppose one of you has 100 sheep, but one of them gets lost.
What will you do? You will leave the other 99 sheep there
in the field and go out and look for the lost sheep.
You will continue to search for it until you find it.
(Luke 15:4, ERV)

The Story: In the story, the little bunny keeps telling his mother that he is going to run away or change to get away from his mother. Each time she assures him that she will do what she needs to so that she can find him and bring him home.

Jesus is like the mother bunny. No matter how much we try to disobey Him and run away from Him, He comes to bring us home.

Think About It:
1. Why does the mother say she will always find the little bunny and bring him home?
2. Is there anywhere little bunny could go to get away from mother bunny?
3. Is there anywhere you can go to get away from God?
4. How does that make you feel?

Your Spirit is everywhere I go.
I cannot escape your presence.
(Psalm 139:7, ERV)

For Further Thought:

1. When you think of the little bunny in the story, how would you describe him?

2. How does his attitude reflect our attitude sometimes as followers of Jesus?

3. Do you ever try to hide from God or hope He doesn't know what you did?

4. Why would someone try to hide from God or run away from Him?

5. Read Psalm 139:1-14. How do those verses make you feel?

Prayer for Today: Dear Jesus, thank You that You are always with me and that You know everything about me. You have known me even before I was born. And You know me now. You know where I am always, and I like that. It makes me feel safe and loved. Sometimes, like the bunny in the story, I want to run away from You because I've done something wrong. Forgive me. Help me to stay close to You always. In Jesus' name, amen.

For Parents: One of the areas that the truth of God's omniscience and omnipresence helps Christians is in repentance. Especially when being accused by Satan when we have sinned, we recognize that nothing is ever hidden from God, He knows all about us from the beginning to end, and nothing we do surprises Him. This truth can help us get back on track when we fail. Instead of dwelling in shame, we can come to our loving Father and admit we sinned and get back in right relationship with God. It does no good to "sew proverbial fig leaves" or "hide behind bushes in the garden." The only answer to sin is confession and acceptance of God's forgiveness. We are never out of His sight, never out of His hands. Wherever we go, He is there. This should comfort us and help us get back into a right relationship quickly.

Another aspect of this is to examine who we are living for. If we are living to please God, knowing that He is always with us and knows everything about us should help give us strength in obedience. Our lives are an expression of our love to God. However, if we are really living to please people and to appear holy, we will probably fall often into temptation and sin. Because when we are away from people, the sense of the need for obedience is also lacking. We may not consciously realize this about ourselves, so we need to pray for God to open our eyes. We need to examine how we act when we are alone or what we think when we see others doing something we disapprove of. Are we judging them even though we smile and say nice things?

The bunny in the story, let's face it, is a bit of a brat. But the mother rabbit persists in loving the bunny anyway and pursues him consistently. God is like that, and unfortunately, sometimes we can be a little bratty ourselves in the way we act, think, and choose.

We want to teach our children to live for God and obey Him. We want them to know He is always with them wherever they go, and that He will never leave them alone. But first, we need to examine our own hearts and see what kind of testimony we are living in front of our children. We should feel loved and secure in God's constant presence, and our children can find that same security in Christ.

Shh! We Have a Plan by Chris Haughton

"LOOK! up there
hello, birdie!
shh SHH! we have a plan."

People might make many plans,
but what the LORD *says is what will happen.*
(Proverbs 19:21, ERV)

The Story: In the story four friends are out in the woods with nets and see a bird. One of them wants to talk to the birdie, but the others keep saying, "Shh, we have a plan." Every time in the story, that is what they tell their friend. But every time their plans fail. It's cute and funny and fun to read.

In real life we make plans too, and sometimes those plans also fail. God says that His plans will never fail.

Think about It:
1. What can we learn about plans from this story?
2. Should the three friends have listened to their other friend? Why or why not?
3. What did the littlest friend do differently than the other three?
4. What does God want us to understand about plans?
5. Why do God's plans never fail?

But the LORD's decisions are good forever.
His plans are good for generation after generation.
(Psalm 33:11, ERV)

For Further Thought:
1. What does the fact that God's plans never fail teach about God?
2. What does it teach us about ourselves?
3. How can we make plans that might succeed?

Prayer for Today: Dear Jesus, I know You have plans for my life, and You have plans for this world. Thank You that we can trust that Your plans and promises are always true. Help me to follow Your plans. I pray You will show me Your plans and help me walk faithfully in them. In Jesus' name, amen.

For the parents: We often feel teaching our children goal setting and reaching objectives is important. Following through on a plan is what will help them become successful adults. This isn't wrong. We just need, as Christian parents, to bring in the reality of God's plans prevailing and bringing our plans under the authority of Christ. He is Lord. His plan matters. Ours need to come under His leadership and plan. This is a lesson in humility, submission, and faith.

If we have teens or young adult children in our homes, talking about goals and God's plan for their lives is a great way to get them thinking about where they are heading in their lives. We can approach the subject without nagging or even suggesting ideas, but we can ask and see where they are and what they are thinking about their futures. In addition, it helps us see how their spiritual maturity is developing. If they haven't been thinking about their futures, this may get them moving on that. It's a great way to remind them that life is more than computer games, selfies, or chatting with friends.

Helping our children set goals can be a fun activity that is also a time of devotion to God and building their faith. Here are some reminders as we begin working through goal setting with our children:

G – Give God Glory: We should give God first priority as we pray with our children about what God is putting on their hearts. As parents, we need to pray for each child as they work through God's plan and calling on their lives. We need to think beyond the surface, self-focused goals we usually think of first, and allow this to become a way we can see God working in our lives, glorifying Himself, and making us more Christlike.

O – Offer Open-Ended Options: We can open up conversations with open-ended questions: We can ask fun questions such as "What if you could accomplish any dream, what would you do?" Or "How could you make a difference in someone's life or show God's love to someone?" And "What do you see God doing around you and in your life?" This will cause our children to think outside the box and onto ideas that could stretch their thinking. With our youngest children, we can ask questions to get them thinking about how God wants them to respond to others and begin building an attitude of seeking God's will and plan in their lives as they grow.

A – Allow for Adaptations: We need to emphasize that goals are not set in stone. This takes away fear and worry. God knows our hearts, and He knows our children's hearts, strengths, and weaknesses. We must allow for updates and changes. Sometimes, it seems that God "fine-tunes" our goals through the process of reaching them. Sometimes they may be long-term goals that cannot be reached in the timeframe we've set. Sometimes God has something a little different in mind than what we originally thought. It's a valuable lesson to teach our children that goals are not set in stone but, as any plan progresses, changes and fine-tuning is a part of the process. Learning that now will serve them well throughout their lives. (I like to use the story of Moses to reiterate this idea. He had a calling, but he took it into his own hands killing an Egyptian soldier. He rushed the plan, acted impulsively based on his feelings, and did not seek God in the matter. After being away for many years, God brings him back to fulfill that originally calling and purpose when Moses is a much humbler, more mature man equipped for the task God has given him).

L – Lead in Logical Lessons: Leading our children to create SMART goals that are Specific, Measurable, Actionable, Relevant, and Timely will help them prepare for success. We can help them set goals that they can check off when completed or can measure how close they come to reaching them. By creating smaller objectives where appropriate and working backwards from the goal to the present time, we can help them see how to move toward their goals and experience success. This will also prevent us and them from giving "Sunday School answers" to goal setting. "God wants me to love everyone" is not a goal. It is an ideal, a value, a belief, but it is not a goal. "God wants me to build a friendship with the new girl in class. I will start by asking her to play four-square at recess this week." That's a goal.

S – Set Up Sensory Signalers: Creating a visual prayer chart for each child, colorful journal, fun magnets for the fridge, or cute notes on the bathroom mirror about the goals serve as reminders to pray about them and work toward them which can help children to focus on what they are working toward. [I hesitate to equate this in any way to a "vision board" since those have the connotation of us using our powers to cause the "universe" to give us stuff (Law of Attraction and New Age thought) So please don't think I am promoting that]. Children are often visual, and having something they can see to pray about each day can help. Set up a prayer list of some kind whether visual or simply a list they see daily, so they can keep praying over these goals and keep them in their hearts and minds.

Areas to Consider

When setting goals, we may want to explore different parts of our lives. We can help our children think through different parts of their lives, different areas in which they may want to set goals. Using Luke 10:27 helps us think through every part of our lives.

The man answered, "'You must love the Lord
your God with all your heart,
all your soul, all your strength, and all your mind.'
And, 'Love your neighbor as yourself.'"
(Luke 10:27, NLT)

- **What are my goals in my family and friendships? (neighbor as yourself)**
- **What are my goals in my education and work? Reading goals? Workshops or learning events I may want to attend? (mind)**
- **What are my physical and health-related goals? Losing weight? Getting in shape? Walking around the block each day? Giving up sodas except for once a week? (strength)**
- **What are my spiritual goals? Read the Bible through in a year? Memorize 100 verses? Spend an hour in prayer each day? (soul)**
- **What are my emotional goals? How can I learn to control my temper? What are some actionable steps for learning to be more loving and kinder? (heart)**

This should be a fun time of self-examination, prayer, and family interaction.

The Thank You Book: An Elephant & Piggie Book
by Mo Willems

Piggie says, "I. Will. Thank. EVERYONE. It will be a THANK-O-RAMA!"

Whatever happens, always be thankful.
This is how God wants you to live in Christ Jesus.
(1 Thessalonians 5:18, ERV)

The Story: This is a cute story where Piggie proclaims he will thank everyone who has been good to him. Elephant warns him he will forget someone important.

Who should get thanks from us every day? That's right! God. We should thank God every day for all He has done for us and for who He is.

Think About It:
1. Have you ever forgotten to say thank you to someone? Did you try to go back and thank the person later?
2. How did each of the animals feel when Piggie thanked them?
3. How do you feel when someone says "Thank you" to you?
4. How do you feel when you feel thankful?
5. Why does God want us to be thankful?
6. How did you feel when Piggie thanked you? Did it make you smile?
7. What do you want to thank God for today?
8. What are some special ways we can express our thanks?
9. What is hard for you to be thankful for?

Give thanks to the LORD because he is good.
His faithful love will last forever.
(1 Chronicles 16:34, ERV)

For Further Thought:

1. The Bible teaches us to always be thankful, but sometimes sad things happen, and we find it hard to be thankful.

2. Do you think God wants us to pretend to be happy about sad things?

3. Can you be thankful for God helping you through the hard times even if you're not always thankful for what happened?

4. Can you be thankful for the friends and family members who help you when you are sad?

5. Does being thankful mean we are thankful and happy about everything that happens?

6. Can you be thankful that hard times and bad things are temporary? They do not last forever.

Prayer for Today: Dear Jesus, thank You for all You have done. Thank You for loving me and saving me. Thank You for my family, my teacher, and my friends. You are so good to me. Thank You for always being with me, day and night, every single day. I love You. In Jesus' name, amen.

For Parents: Thankfulness is one of those traits we all want to build into our children's lives. It creates people who realize how blessed they are, who can find contentment in life, and who understand the beauty of generosity. Thankfulness also shifts our thinking from what we don't have to what we've been blessed with. We usually begin with teaching our children to say "Thank you" to those who give them things and in our prayers for food or whatever God blesses us with. But having a heart and mind filled with gratitude is a character quality that will serve our children well throughout their lives. We can incorporate several activities each year to help our kids become aware of opportunities for gratitude.

Here are a few simple ideas:

Create a thankfulness wall where family members write down items of thanksgiving or answered prayers.

Between Thanksgiving and Christmas, create a Thanksgiving Tree where notes of gratitude can be hung on each branch.

On the way to school each day or on the way home from church each week, spend time sharing what each family member is thankful for.

Create a counting book of blessings.

Express our gratitude for each child, especially on their birthdays each year.

The Very Impatient Caterpillar by **Ross Burach**

"Am I a butterfly yet?"
"No."
"How about now?"
"No."
"Now?"
"No. Be patient!"

It is better to finish something than to start it.
It is better to be gentle and patient than to be proud and impatient.
(Ecclesiastes 7:8, ERV)

The Story: In this story the caterpillar is so excited to be changed into a butterfly. He understands what a miracle that is. He can't wait! But he must.

Waiting is hard. Letting God change us is hard like the caterpillar waiting to change into a butterfly. We must be patient. God is at work in us, making us more like Jesus. God is at work through us, helping us share His love with us. God is at work around us, working all thing together for our good for those of us who serve Him.

Think About It:

1. What is happening in the story that makes it hard for the caterpillar to wait?

2. What does it mean to be patient?

3. Did his questioning and complaining help the process to go faster?

4. When do you find it hard to be patient?

People might make many plans,
but what the LORD says is what will happen.
(Proverbs 19:21, ERV)

For Further Thought:
1. Do you think it's hard to wait?
2. Do you ever get impatient with God?
3. Do you believe He has a plan and is working it out in your life?
4. What is the worst thing you've had to wait for?
5. How is God working through your life?
6. Do you know that He is always working and helping us to grow in our faith?
7. Are there ways you could let Him work more through your life to bless others?

Prayer for Today: Dear Jesus, help me in the waiting times. I know You are working in my life to make me more like Jesus. I know that Your timing is right for when everything happens. I just need to trust You and wait patiently. Help me be peaceful and patient as I wait. In Jesus' name, amen.

For Parents: Patience in this story is about development and letting God work out in His timing the changes in our lives. Often with our children, we allow certain activities at certain ages: riding a bicycle in the street, getting a cell phone, or going to a friend's house after school for example. Helping our children understand that waiting is important and that we know what is best and when it is best is a matter of trust and respect from our kids.

Sometimes simply talking with them about the plan can help. That shows that we trust them enough for them to understand that we have their best interest at heart. Helping them see the freedom we are giving them as they develop will help too. They will see that little by little they are becoming independent and that we trust them with that freedom.

Of course, when they break our trust in these things, we have the opportunity to talk about how maybe they aren't quite mature enough for what we thought they were. We can hold off on a certain freedom a little longer until they are ready. This adds the understanding of responsibility with freedom and waiting until the right timing.

With very young children, this may be as simple as letting them pour their own milk or get their own juice box. It may involve letting them decide between two choices: what to wear or where to go, for instance. This gives them autonomy within appropriate boundaries and helps them learn responsibility early.

I've seen parents do this so gracefully. We use the analogy of apron strings holding our children to us. The parents who help their children gracefully find independence, responsibility, and critical thinking are loosening the apron strings in tiny steps in each stage of development. So, then, when they are in their teen years, we've established the importance of trust and responsibility. We can more easily let out the apron strings a little more until they are ready to go out on their own. All the while, they have learned patience and to trust our wisdom. This can transfer into their understanding of God and how He works in our lives.

Waiting Is Not Easy! By Mo Willems

"I CANNOT WAIT!" [said Gerald]
"You will have to." [said Piggie]

*Wait for the LORD's help. Be strong and brave,
and wait for the LORD's help. (Psalm 27:14, ERV)*

The Story: Gerald has a hard time waiting. He is so excited for the surprise Piggie has for him. Piggie knows Gerald will be happy he waited, but Gerald is still impatient. In the end, they agree it was worth the wait.

We get impatient too. When we know we are getting a present or are going to the zoo, we can be impatient not wanting to wait. Like Gerald said, "It is not easy to wait!" But sometimes we must.

We pray asking God for help, and then we may need to wait. Waiting can be hard. But it is worth the wait if we will be patient. When we follow Jesus, we know that someday we will be in heaven where we will have no more pain, no more tears, and everything will be perfect. But for now, we must wait. When we trust God, it is easier to wait. When we are patient, we wait peacefully.

Think About It:
1. Do you ever wonder why we must wait for things?
2. Why do you think God sometimes has us wait for answers to our prayers?
3. Do you like waiting?
4. Do you trust God that if it is good for you to have something, He will give it to you?
5. Do you think you will feel happy when you get what you're waiting for?

*Hope that is delayed makes you sad,
but a wish that comes true fills you with joy.
(Proverbs 13:12, ERV)*

Another verse talks about how we wait, hoping for God's promises to be fulfilled. When we follow Christ and believe in Him as our Lord and Savior, we have His promise that we will live forever with Him in heaven. But for now, we wait. We hope. We are patient.

But we are hoping for something we don't have yet,
and we are waiting for it patiently.
(Romans 8:25, ERV)

For Further Thought:
1. What prayer are you waiting for God to answer?
2. What is hardest for you to wait for?
3. Can God help you be more patient?
4. Do you trust God even if the answer is "no"?
5. Do you believe God's yes is worth the wait?

Prayer for Today: Dear Jesus, I don't like waiting, but I am glad You help me grow up more when I wait. I am learning to trust You more. I am learning to be patient. I am learning to hold on to hope instead of getting mad. Help me, Lord. Sometimes it's so hard to wait. I trust You and wait. In Jesus' name, amen.

For Parents: Patience, a trait we all wish our children (and we) can learn. Admittedly, developing patience is often a painful endeavor. It usually requires waiting or dealing with difficulties that we want to change.

Ways we can help our children learn patience is:

1. Delay gratification – Having children sit and color quietly while we fix lunch or having them help us prepare a meal so they can see the process can help develop patience and the ability to wait. Plus, they see how working toward something can help them get what they want.

2. Plan for and save for something.

3. The toughest times for patience are when tired or hungry. Talking about it and helping them learn self-control is important. When we show we understand they are tired or hungry, but we ask them to show self-control and praise them for doing a good job of self-control when they do helps them internalize the discipline of patience.

4. Take turns. For instance, on a long car trip, each child gets a turn to choose the movie they watch or game they play. Finding opportunities for taking turns is a great way to teach patience and gracious waiting.

Similarly, children need to learn to graciously accept no as an answer. Ironically, one of the best ways to get a child to accept a no answer is to often say yes. When children know we have their best interest at heart, that we don't say no constantly, and that we enjoy blessing them when appropriate, they are often more willing to accept a no. We need to help them learn to accept the no graciously and with patience. We need to tell them what we expect from them. We tell them begging is wrong, asking after we say no is not acceptable, and whining is never okay. When we say no, with some children, it is important to explain why we are saying no, but they should also understand if we do not want to explain. We must help our children understand that trusting us in enough. It is the same with trusting God in His answers. If we know ahead of time that we are going to be in a situation where the child will want something they cannot have, we can prepare them for that situation and the "no" ahead of time.

We Don't Eat Our Classmates by Ryan T. Higgins

"Once Penelope found out what it was like to be someone's snack, she lost her appetite for children."

Try to do what is good for others, not just what is good for yourselves.
(1 Corinthians 10:24, ERV)

The Story: Penelope has a difficult time going to a new school, especially since she is a T-Rex, and she was going to school with human children. At first, she found it hard to be friends because she saw them as snacks, and they saw her as, well, a T-Rex! The second day of school she really wanted to make friends, but she still wasn't thinking about how she was scaring the children. Then, suddenly things changed. She understood, and she began to be a real friend to the children.

We talk a lot about "Treat others the way you want to be treated." But we also need to think about how what we do affects others. The Bible tells us to be friendly and kind to others. We are to try to do what is good for others, not just what is good for us it says in 1 Corinthians 10:24. Jesus taught us to love God and love others.

Think About It:
1. When Penelope ate her classmates, how did her teacher and the children feel?
2. What happened to help Penelope understand how the children felt?
3. How could you try to understand how someone else feels?
4. How could you make a new student feel welcomed in your class?

One law rules over all other laws. This royal law is found in the Scriptures: "Love your neighbor the same as you love yourself." If you obey this law, you are doing right.
(James 2:8, ERV)

For Further Thought:
1. What does it mean to love your neighbor as yourself?
2. How would your actions change if you did this every day?
3. How could you be a better friend to someone you've had a hard time being friends with?

Prayer for Today: Dear Jesus, help me to see what others need. Help me to bless them and do what is good for them. Help me to not always only think about myself. Thank you. In Jesus' name, amen.

For Parents: As we know, friends have a profound impact on our children's lives. Bullying can cause fear and anxiety. We want to raise children who love others and are good friends to others, but we also want our children to make good choices in the friends they choose.

As you go through this devotional, it might open the door to talk about your child's classmates or friends at church. Who is a good friend? Why do you say they are a good friend? Who is not such a good friend? Why? How have you been a good friend to others?

If they go to friends' houses, ask how they feel at each friend's house. What is different in one place from the other?

We never want to lead our children into fear or create problems, but we want to know if there are problems or a need for concern. Asking open-ended questions and letting them share how they feel is important. Listening to what they are saying is vital. A child may hide that he or she is being bullied or hurt. Sometimes children can pick up on clues that someone is not trustworthy, yet we try to make them be friendly toward everyone. Listen to your children. Ask why they don't care for a certain person. It may be that they don't like the person's hair, but it could be that they don't like the way the person treats them or a sibling.

When I was young, I had an uncle who did not respect anything I said. If I said no, he ignored it. He never tried anything inappropriate with me, but he never respected me either. All I could say to my mom was, "I said no, and he swung me around anyway. I hated it." I hated it because I felt violated and disrespected. I felt like a non-human. This same uncle went much further with my cousin. I may have been sensing something wasn't right with this man. But for sure, I sensed that he did not respect me, and I didn't feel safe around him.

Whether we're talking about an adult friend or a child friend, we need to hear our children's hearts and help them navigate their friendships. We won't be able to protect them from every mean comment or impolite person in the world, and we shouldn't, but we can help them know how to respond to others when they are unkind or hurtful. And knowing as much as we can, maybe we can protect them from the really bad stuff that's out in the world and sometimes visiting in our homes.

You Should, You Should! By Ginny Tilby

"You look hungry. Come and eat!
You should *peck-peck-peck* this treat.
A hippo's *CHOMP* is dull and dreary.
Peck-peck-peck is bright and cheery!"
"Don't chomp? Okay. I should obey.
I want you to like me.
I'll *peck-peck* away."

> *God has made us what we are. In Christ Jesus,*
> *God made us new people so that we would spend our*
> *lives doing the good things he had already planned for us to do.*
> *(Ephesians 2:10, ERV)*

The Story: Hippo starts out his day well, but then each animal tells him he's doing things wrong. Hippo should be like them. Hippo is what we call a "people pleaser"—someone who wants people to like him, so he changes what he's like to try to fit in.

God creates each person with unique abilities, and He wants us to be who He created us to be. That means we must know what the Bible says and obey it. We can love others, but we don't need to mimic them or try to be just like them. God has a plan for your life and for each person's life. We honor God when we live life loving and obeying God.

Think About It:

1. Do you think God wants us to imitate others or live our lives the way He created us?

2. Why do you think all the other animals were trying to make Hippo act like them?

3. How could his friends have really helped him?

4. Some things in life are right or wrong. Some things can be done many different ways, and none of them are right or wrong; they are just different. How can we tell the difference?

84

Be humble before the Lord, and he will make you great.
Brothers and sisters, don't say anything against each other.
If you criticize your brother or sister in Christ or judge them,
you are criticizing and judging the law they follow.
And when you are judging the law, you are not a follower
of the law. You have become a judge. God is the one who
gave us the law, and he is the Judge.
He is the only one who can save and destroy.
So it is not right for you to judge anyone.
(James 4:10-12, ERV)

For Further Thought:

1. Should we give advice when we don't know what we're talking about?

2. When someone does something differently than we do, sometimes we think they are doing it wrong. Have you ever judged someone in this way?

3. Were they wrong or just different?

4. How could we show grace and understanding to someone who is different from us?

5. How could you encourage someone who is afraid to be themselves?

Prayer for Today: Dear Jesus, I know that You created me and everyone in the world to be unique people even though we are all created in Your image. I know it means everyone is important to You. You love each one of us. Thank You for that. Help me to appreciate other people and their unique ways of doing things so that I do not judge others in a mean way. Help me to be kind. In Jesus' name, amen.

For Parents: Today, any time a book talks about differences and respecting differences, the topic of transgender and LGBTQ will often come up. I do not believe that is what this book is about, but it could be taken there.

Humility and kindness are important traits we should all have, practice, and teach to our children. Helping our kids know right from wrong yet helping them understand they don't have to try to change others is tough. Little ones have such a sense of justice. If they see someone doing wrong, they often want to jump in and tell the person he or she is wrong. But sometimes that is not appropriate.

One big issue facing our little ones today in our culture is the transgender phenomenon. I won't go into how troubling and truly evil the activists are being to our children. Here, we are only concerned with how to help our children in these situations. If a friend insists on being treated like a boy when she is a girl, how should our children respond. It is very confusing and troubling for most children, especially our 4–7 year olds. How can they respond with kindness when they know something is wrong? Helping our children handle this is important. For some, it causes great anxiety. You may want to practice a conversation with your child and help him or her know how to respond.

We need to pray. So many young people are being hurt by this phenomenon, and it is causing young people to hurt themselves. This whole situation is sexualizing children at a very young age. It is confusing. It is terrifying to some children. We need to tell our children the truth, and we need to help them feel empowered with kindness while confident in the truth. This will help them find some peace in this terrible situation.

Made in the USA
Columbia, SC
23 December 2023

29378136R00050